SERIES EDITOR Thomas S. C. Farrell

Curriculum Design in English Language Teaching

Ilka Kostka

Lucy Bunning

www.tesol.org/bookstore

TESOL International Association
1925 Ballenger Avenue
Alexandria, Virginia, 22314 USA
www.tesol.org

Director of Publishing and Product Development: Myrna Jacobs
Copy Editor: Sarah Duffy
Cover: Citrine Sky Design
Interior Design & Layout: Capitol Communications, LLC

Copyright © 2018 by TESOL International Association

All rights reserved. Copying or further publication of the contents of this work are not permitted without permission of TESOL International Association, except for limited "fair use" for educational, scholarly, and similar purposes as authorized by U.S. Copyright Law, in which case appropriate notice of the source of the work should be given. Permission to reproduce material from this book must be obtained from www.copyright.com, or contact Copyright Clearance Center, Inc., 222 Rosewood Drive, Danvers, MA 01923, 978-750-8400.

Every effort has been made to contact copyright holders for permission to reprint borrowed material. We regret any oversights that may have occurred and will rectify them in future printings of this work.

ISBN 978-1-942799-96-2
Library of Congress Control Number 2017954015

Table of Contents

Series Editor's Preface v

Chapter 1: Introduction 1

Chapter 2: The Six Ws and an H of Curriculum Design 3

Chapter 3: From Needs Analysis to Curriculum Design 11

Chapter 4: From Curriculum Design to Implementation 21

Chapter 5: From Implementation to Evaluation 29

Chapter 6: Recommendations and Conclusion 37

References 41

Series Editor's Preface

The English Language Teacher Development (ELTD) series consists of a set of short resource books for ESOL teachers that are written in a jargon-free and accessible manner for all types of teachers of English (native, nonnative, experienced, and novice teachers). The ELTD series is designed to offer teachers a theory-to-practice approach to second language teaching, and each book offers a wide variety of practical teaching approaches and methods related to the topic at hand. Each book also offers time for reflections for each teacher to interact with the materials presented in the book. The books can be used in preservice settings or in in-service courses and can also be used by individuals looking for ways to refresh their practice.

In *Curriculum Design*, Ilka Kostka and Lucy Bunning explore various methods and approaches for how knowledge of curriculum design can inform language teaching. They show how curriculum is a multilayered process. The book moves from needs analysis to curriculum design, to implementation, and finally to evaluation of the curriculum. The authors also include their own experiences and reflections with curriculum design, sharing what they learned along the way. *Curriculum Design* is another valuable addition to the literature in our profession and to the ELTD series.

I am very grateful to the authors who contributed to the ELTD series for sharing their knowledge and expertise with other TESOL professionals. It is truly an honor for me to work with each of these authors as they selflessly give their valuable time for the advancement of TESOL.

Thomas S. C. Farrell

CHAPTER 1

Introduction

Curriculum design involves creating, implementing, and evaluating a curriculum, which is "the overall plan or design for a course and how the content for a course is transformed into a blueprint for teaching and learning which enables the desired learning outcomes to be achieved" (Richards, 2013, p. 6). Because curriculum design directly impacts teaching and learning and shapes students' success, it is an important element of English language teaching. Many English language teachers contribute to curriculum design in some way over the course of their teaching careers and thus can benefit from an understanding of the processes that are involved in it.

The aim of this book is to provide readers with an introduction to curriculum design. In Chapter 2, we offer a broad overview of the key components involved in designing a curriculum. In Chapter 3, we take readers through the process of needs analysis, highlighting the work involved in using needs analysis data to design a curriculum. In Chapter 4, we shift the focus from curriculum design to implementation, focusing on the factors and decisions involved in teaching and administering a curriculum. In Chapter 5, we describe how to evaluate an implemented curriculum and use the results to inform future changes. In Chapter 6, we conclude by reflecting on our own experiences with curriculum design to offer recommendations for embarking on the process. Each chapter includes several reflective questions, which we encourage readers to think about and discuss with colleagues. While we acknowledge there is not one single best approach to curriculum design, our short book aims to present readers with the most fundamental processes that underlie it.

> **REFLECTION QUESTIONS**
>
> - What do you already know about curriculum design? What do you want to learn more about?

CHAPTER 2

The Six Ws and an H of Curriculum Design

Curriculum design involves a number of different variables, all of which are situated within a particular educational context. In this chapter, we ask and answer seven basic questions to introduce each of these variables. Identifying the main elements of curriculum design is useful for understanding the role they play within larger parts of the process described later in this book, such as needs analysis, design, implementation, and evaluation.

> **REFLECTIVE QUESTION**
>
> - Imagine you are about to begin designing the curriculum at your institution. Write down as many factors as you can think of that would play a role in the design process. Why should curriculum designers identify these before beginning the curriculum design process?

What Is Curriculum Design?

Simply defined, curriculum design is the process of working on an informed plan for teaching and learning, and it is an essential undertaking wherever English is taught and learned in an organized setting. These settings might include an intensive English program, a primary or secondary school, a university pathway program, or an adult education program, among others. During the curriculum design process, instructors, administrators, and stakeholders work together to identify their particular program's mission and goals and learners' needs. They can then develop a framework for what will be the focus and organization, or scope and sequence, of teaching and learning. In this way, they situate their curriculum design in the local context in which learning is taking place. Once they implement the new curriculum, they can begin evaluating it and making adjustments if necessary.

The stages in the curriculum design process that we describe in each chapter of this book are illustrated in Figure 1. The starting point is the unique curriculum task to accomplish or question to answer, but as you can see, there is no clear end point.

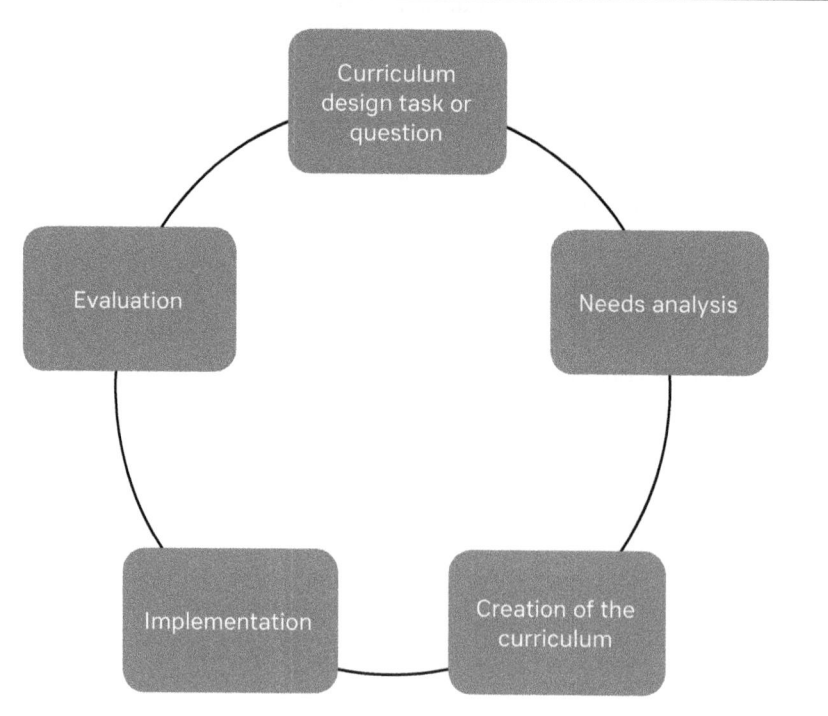

Figure 1. The Process of Curriculum Design Outlined in This Book

As the figure shows, each phase connects to the next phase, and curriculum designers might revisit the previous stage if needed. For instance, if the design task is to develop a curriculum for a new language school, the designers would likely first conduct a needs analysis and then create the curriculum to be implemented and then evaluated and revised. Alternatively, if the design task is to update an existing curriculum, the designers might begin with an evaluation of the curriculum coupled with a needs analysis and then create the revised curriculum. Thinking of curriculum design as a nonlinear process can help those involved maintain flexibility and a mindset that is geared toward improvement rather than completion.

REFLECTIVE QUESTION

- What effect might skipping any of these stages have on the curriculum?

What Are Different Approaches to Curriculum Design?

There are many approaches to curriculum design, each of which depends on the overall goal of the curriculum. In their comprehensive book, Christison and Murray (2014) outline four different approaches. The first is a *linguistic-based* curriculum, which is organized around language features such as grammatical structures, genres, language functions, and/or language skills. The second is a *content-based* curriculum, where language instruction takes place in relation to specific subject matter. The linguistic demands of the subject matter or content determine which aspects of language are taught. The third approach is a *learner-centered* curriculum, which prioritizes the process of language learning. In this type of curriculum, learners contribute to decision making about what to learn and how to go about it. They might also complete projects that require them to engage in authentic tasks. Finally, a *learning-centered* curriculum focuses on the product of what is to be learned or the outcome that students will be able to produce, which is often expressed in terms of outcomes, competencies, or standards. While each approach is valuable in its own right, choosing one over the other will depend on the setting, students, and purpose of the language program.

REFLECTIVE QUESTIONS

- Christison and Murray (2014) offer examples of each of the four curriculum design approaches they describe (i.e., linguistic-based, content-based, learner-centered, and learning-centered). Look at each of the examples below and determine which approach each best exemplifies. What factors influenced your choices? Where do you see overlap among the approaches?

    — An ESL course is attached to an information technology course that supports immigrant and refugee students who do not have documentation of the prerequisites for the information technology certificate program.

    — An elementary or secondary school relies on TESOL International Association's (2006) PreK–12 English Language Proficiency standards that define types of communication students need to be successful in school. Also provided are descriptors of behaviors that meet the standard as well as progress indicators to guide students' language development accordingly.

    — A U.S. history course is part of an intensive English program in which students have a choice of either creating a midterm exam to administer to classmates, writing a research paper, or proposing an original project. All of these assignments require students to create and complete a rubric to evaluate their work.

    — In a four-level intensive English program, each level targets a specific range of grammatical structures.

Why Is Effective Curriculum Design Important?

Because curriculum design directly affects learning, it is essential that all of the varying parts of the design relate directly to the learners (Nation & Macalister, 2010). This is particularly important when there is limited time for students to accomplish their goals. For instance, students in a pathways program may have only one or two academic terms to improve their English before matriculating to a university. Similarly, a businessperson preparing for a trip to a branch location in an English-speaking country may have only a few weeks to learn basic English communication skills before embarking on a trip. An effective curriculum is also important when a language program includes multiple years of study. For instance, when English is taught as a foreign language throughout elementary and secondary school, a clear plan for how the instruction will progress can help keep teachers and students on track. In these situations and in others, a properly established curriculum is crucial for maximizing the chances of student success and perhaps even the success of the program and institution.

Effective curriculum design can also ensure that the many variables involved in teaching and learning align. These variables may include the following:

- teaching materials (e.g., books, technology, course management software)
- human resources (e.g., staff, instructors, students, stakeholders, administrators, advisers)
- classroom and program policies (e.g., the use of English in class, attendance)
- scheduling and amount of time available for instruction
- instructors' professional knowledge and development
- instructors' principles and beliefs about language teaching and learning

All of these elements, informed by a needs analysis and research on curriculum design practices, provide a foundation upon which the curriculum is established.

Who Is Involved in Curriculum Design and Why?

Curriculum design typically involves a number of individuals. First, teachers play an important role in contributing to the curriculum because they are directly impacted by curriculum changes. As Carroll (2007) noted, "If teachers are excluded from all involvement in the direction of the change processes, they may in fact be not so much unwilling as unable to implement it effectively" (p. 5). In addition, learners themselves may become involved in curriculum design as they provide feedback about a course (either formally or informally) and their learning outcomes are evaluated.

Other stakeholders may provide input into curriculum design as well. For example, people who will interact with language program graduates (e.g., other educators, coworkers, employers) may have valuable perspectives to offer about desirable competencies and students' preparedness. Additionally, language program administrators may become involved in curriculum design, bringing their knowledge of institutional policies and regulations. All of these people can offer key insights into the processes of designing and implementing a new curriculum because they are invested in student success.

Where Is a Language Curriculum Put Into Place?

A curriculum can be used wherever teaching and learning occurs. These settings may include nonprofit organizations, classes offered in the workplace, schools, universities, private or for-profit language programs, and individualized settings such as private tutoring sessions and online self-study courses. Within these settings, there are many possible sources of curricula, including a government's department of education, a professional organization or governing body, a school, a program, or a publisher. A language teacher can also develop his or her own curriculum for or with students that is situated within the local context and based on students' unique needs, as we describe in Chapter 3.

When Is a Curriculum Established?

A curriculum is created whenever there is a need to organize instruction and achieve learning outcomes. In some situations, teachers may implement a curriculum during the course of instruction if no formal curriculum has been previously established. This might entail negotiating the course syllabus or curriculum in collaboration with learners throughout a course and/or adjusting their teaching in response to students' needs and lacks. In other situations, stakeholders and instructors may create a curriculum in response to a particular need that arises. For example, Japan will host the Olympic and Paralympic Games in 2020 and expects to attract nearly

40 million tourists, thus there is a demand for instructors and tutors of English and other languages to help locals welcome visitors and provide logistical, medical, and linguistic support during the Games (Kikuchi, 2017). As these situations show, a curriculum can be established and implemented at any time.

How Do Different Stages of Curriculum Design Interplay?

As we mentioned earlier in this chapter, the general process of curriculum design involves a series of interrelated steps that often overlap. For instance, Brown and Lee (2015) describe a 4-week summer course developed for students from a university in Central America who were visiting the United States. Brown and his colleagues conducted both a needs analysis and a situation analysis to learn more about the students' goals and the available resources at the receiving university. They then used the information gathered to create the curriculum for the course, drawing on a published textbook and an existing curriculum from the institution. When students arrived, it quickly became evident that changes would need to be made to the curriculum based on low enrollment, lower proficiency levels, and different learning priorities. Brown and his colleagues thus promptly revised their plan and managed to create a memorable course and experience for the students. This example illustrates how the different stages of curriculum design interplay and affect one another.

> **REFLECTIVE QUESTIONS**
>
> - Talk to someone you know who is involved in a language program. In their opinion, which factors are most important in designing a curriculum? How do their answers align with the general overview of the process provided in this chapter?

CHAPTER 3

From Needs Analysis to Curriculum Design

An effective curriculum is one that is both directly connected to the goals and needs of students and relevant to the environment in which the curriculum is established. Taking students' needs into account is essential because it ensures that the curriculum will be useful to them as they progress toward their learning goals (Nation & Macalister, 2010). In this chapter, we discuss the process of conducting a needs analysis, focusing on different approaches and how instructors and stakeholders can use the data collected to inform curriculum design.

> **REFLECTIVE QUESTIONS**
> - Consider the following scenario. Undergraduate international students in an intensive English program must obtain a certain score on an English proficiency exam to pass the program and matriculate to the university. Because this is a high-stakes exam, many students believe that preparing for this exam is more important than attending classes, and they often skip class to memorize test questions and study on their own. How might what students think they need differ from what teachers and stakeholders believe students need? How would you manage those differences?

What Is a Needs Analysis?

A needs analysis refers to "procedures used to collect information about learners' needs" (Richards, 2001, p. 51). Nation and Macalister (2010) offer a useful model of needs analysis that categorizes needs into three types: needs, lacks, and wants. They begin by stating that *needs* can be determined by asking, "What is necessary in the learners' use of language?" (p. 24). For instance, graduate students in a pathway program may need to learn how to write research-based papers before matriculating to their degree programs. Nation and Macalister then define *lacks* as the knowledge and skills that students do not presently have, which may include skills that they have not acquired while learning either their first or second language. Information about students' lacks may come from the learners themselves, their instructors, or the work students have produced in the target language. Finally, Nation and Macalister define *wants* as learners' own ideas about what they believe will help them learn. It is important to note that while students' wishes may not align perfectly with what teachers know about best practices, knowing what students want to learn can help teachers either address this difference or adapt their courses to satisfy students' wants.

> **REFLECTIVE QUESTION**
>
> - What are the students' needs, lacks, and wants in the curriculum that you teach?

One of the most important implications of a needs analysis is that it is practical and should be used to directly inform curriculum change. Richards (2001) offers several reasons for conducting a needs analysis:

- determining the skills students need in their particular settings and whether current courses fulfill those needs
- identifying differences between students' current language skills and target goals
- determining potential curriculum changes
- pinpointing and examining existing problems
- gathering information about challenges learners are facing

Richards continues to say that knowing *why* a needs analysis must be done is an important first step in conducting one. Curriculum designers need to ask themselves what kinds of information they want to obtain from the needs analysis and what the information will be used for. For instance, data may be used to evaluate a language program, develop teaching materials and assessments, or fulfill requirements for external funding. While a needs analysis is typically the first step in curriculum design, it can be conducted whenever information is needed about learners; this may be before, during, or after instruction takes place.

Various types of data are collected to provide information, and as Richards (2001) notes, the more information that is gathered, the better. Data may include questionnaires given to current and former students in a language program; existing course syllabi and materials; interviews with teachers, students, staff, and policy-makers; students' test scores; classroom observations; and market research about similar language programs.

While it is important to conduct a needs analysis that takes a specific local context into account, curriculum designers can also make use of larger frameworks and standards that have already been established. Some well-known examples of these frameworks include the *Common European Framework of Reference for Languages* (Council of Europe, 2001), *2012 Amplification of the English Language Development Standards* (WIDA, 2012), and *Massachusetts ABE Curriculum Framework for English for Speakers of Other Languages* (Massachusetts Department of Education, 2005). Although they are not geared toward a particular curriculum, they are helpful in guiding the progression of language development and providing a structure upon which to build a more localized curriculum.

The Local Environment

After curriculum designers perform a needs analysis, they must also consider the environment in which they are teaching. This process is what Richards (2001) calls a *situation analysis* and what Nation and Macalister (2010) call an *environment analysis*. A situation analysis parallels a needs analysis because it examines "the factors in the context of a planned or present curriculum project that is made in order to assess their potential impact on the project. These factors may be political, social, economic, or institutional" (Richards, 2001, p. 91). In other words, a situation analysis considers the larger domain in which a curriculum is situated, and when it is performed as part of a needs analysis, it can help prevent difficulties and frustration when a new curriculum is implemented (Richards, 2001).

Richards (2001) notes that some of the elements that may be included in a situation analysis may be related to society at large (e.g., views about language learning held by the local culture, government, and employers), the institutional culture and methods of operation, members of the situation analysis project (e.g., levels of expertise, leadership skills), allotted time and resources, teachers (e.g., language proficiency, teaching experience, beliefs, training), learners (e.g., prior language learning backgrounds, motivation levels, preferences for particular instructional styles), and adoption (e.g., how curricular changes are perceived and integrated). Neglecting these elements could have a negative influence on the effectiveness of the curriculum.

REFLECTIVE QUESTIONS

- Think of an example of a language program that would benefit from a situation analysis. What are some possible reasons curriculum designers might ignore situational factors? What are possible consequences of this type of neglect?

An Example of a Needs Analysis: Rwanda

Consider a needs analysis that one of the authors conducted to create a content-based curriculum for a private security company in Rwanda. Employees needed English because they regularly interacted with visitors from around the world, and English was the shared language they used to communicate. This English course was optional for employees, yet many of them wanted to enroll in it to both demonstrate their commitment to the employer and take advantage of a valuable opportunity to develop their English language skills. A pre-course needs analysis included the components in Table 1.

Table 1. Needs Analysis Conducted for an English Course in Rwanda

Questions	Data collected
• When do the security personnel need to use English at work? • How often do they need to use English? • Who do they need to interact with? • Why do they want to learn English?	• Conversations with the employer and security personnel to determine likely situations for English use • Observations of their interactions at work
• What tasks do security personnel need to accomplish in English? • Which vocabulary and grammatical structures do they need to use?	• Observations of security personnel at work to examine features of their communication, vocabulary, and grammatical structures
• What kinds of resources (e.g., books, technology) are available to support teaching and learning? • How much time is allotted for instruction?	• Meetings with stakeholders
• What are local views about English language learning? For instance, what do language teachers in this context believe about language learning? • What status does English have in the local community and in the country? How might that affect this curriculum?	• Interviews with potential teachers • Information about the community from teachers
• Are the security personnel at beginning stages of English language development or more advanced learners?	• Impressions of the employer based on his interactions with employees • Self-evaluation on the first day of class

The results of the needs analysis were used to develop materials for students to practice the English needed to carry out work-related responsibilities, plan class activities, identify appropriate teaching methods, and divide the security personnel into two groups. Gathering information about the needs of this particular group of learners, the resources available, and the learning context increased the potential for the English course to address learners' needs.

> **REFLECTIVE QUESTIONS**
>
> - The needs analysis in Rwanda accomplished its aim; however, there is room for improvement. Consider this example and what you have read about conducting a needs analysis. What would you like to find out about students' proficiency levels, strengths, formal education background, and native language literacy skills? What types of data would help you answer those questions?

Approaches to Needs Analysis

Just as there are different approaches to the process of curriculum design, there are also varying approaches to conducting a needs analysis. For instance, in a curriculum that includes multiple courses for a progression of proficiency levels, curriculum designers would want to ensure that the objectives for the various courses in one level complement one another in terms of language, content, and activities. Objectives should also align from one level to the next in a logical sequence. One approach to this process is using Wiggins and McTighe's (2005) principle of backward design, in which they "identify desired results, determine acceptable evidence, [and] plan learning experiences and instruction" (p. 18). Although steps two and three likely take place at the instructional level rather than the curriculum design level, step one is key to curriculum design and subsequent teaching and learning. The rationale behind this approach is that the destination must be first identified in order to determine how to get there and whether the destination is reached.

In contrast to using backward design to align objectives across courses and levels, other approaches to needs analysis and curriculum design emphasize dynamic decision making. For instance, Auerbach (1992) advocates for a participatory approach that prioritizes the learning of each unique group of learners rather than the status quo of predetermined outcomes or competencies. In her approach, the curriculum design and needs analysis processes start with learners and emerge over time as they work together with teachers to identify issues that are important to them. Lee's (2014) study of North Korean refugees learning English in South Korea provides an example of a participatory curriculum. Lee compared the mainstream English curriculum used in Korea and a participatory curriculum that was implemented based on students' needs. Findings show that while the mainstream curriculum did not fit North Korean learners' needs and discouraged them from learning, the participatory curriculum was effective in engaging them in their learning and empowering them to challenge negative stereotypes that had been ascribed to them. Lee's work highlights the impact of contextualizing a curriculum and actively involving students in the course design process.

In other circumstances, a needs analysis is performed when stakeholders want to improve a part of an existing curriculum. For instance, Caplan and Stevens (2017) describe how a needs analysis was conducted at their university in the United States to revise part of an English for academic purposes (EAP) curriculum in their intensive English program (IEP). The first step taken was determining what international students at their school needed and wanted to learn as well as which areas they needed improvement in. Data included information from a survey completed by current students, matriculated undergraduate international students at the university, and university faculty, as well as interviews with five students who successfully completed the program. This needs analysis helped to uncover the challenges that international students faced and helped the authors make changes to their curriculum to address students' linguistic and cultural challenges, among others. For example, a new integrated skills course was created in their program to help meet these needs and address the concerns that both faculty and students had about international students' preparation for academic study in the United States. Caplan and Stevens's work provides a strong example of how a needs analysis can directly and positively lead to curriculum changes.

REFLECTIVE QUESTIONS

- Think about a curriculum in which you have either taught or studied. What was its overall goal? How were the sequencing and content of lessons or courses designed to help students reach this goal?

From Needs Analysis to Curriculum Design

Once data have been collected through a needs and situation analysis, curriculum designers can move to the next step of using the data to work on the curriculum itself. A practical way to begin is to compile all of the data in one place, either in paper or electronic format, and ensure that everyone working on the curriculum has access to it.

Curriculum designers then need to collaborate to interpret all of this information and figure out which needs should be prioritized (Richards, 2001). At this stage, it is helpful to develop questions that remain unanswered and to examine the existing curriculum (if there is one) to determine whether these prioritized needs are currently being met. Throughout the process of interpreting data, teachers, staff, administrators, and/or stakeholders may want to offer their own analyses of the data and share their viewpoints. Curriculum designers can compile the data they have collected into a report or summary, which may then be shared with stakeholders and teachers. Once they compile the data, they can also use it for multiple purposes, such as planning instruction and courses, revising existing parts of a curriculum, making decisions about the curriculum, and informing a program's goals and objectives (Richards, 2001).

Standardized Testing in the Curriculum

A high-stakes standardized English proficiency test is sometimes required of students either before they move on to their next steps or as they conclude their studies. In academic settings, this test could be either the TOEFL (Test of English as a Foreign Language) or IELTS (International English Language Testing System). In workplace settings, the TOEIC (Test of English for International Communication) may be used to measure students' proficiency. Adult education settings in the United States often use BEST (Basic English Skills Test) or CASAS (Comprehensive Adult Student Assessment Systems) tests. Although standardized testing is controversial, it remains a reality in many language learning contexts.

The relationship between standardized tests and language program curriculum is worthy of consideration (Cumming, 2009). For instance, if the name of a course is "TOEFL Preparation," it is likely that there is a very close relationship between the course outcomes, materials, class activities, and the

TOEFL. However, if a standardized high-stakes test is required of learners, but is not a specific goal of the course, curriculum designers, teachers, administrators, and students will need to make decisions about how much test content and preparation are included. These factors must be considered when a curriculum is being designed, and a needs analysis can help curriculum designers make connections between the test and the instructional methods that are used to prepare students for it.

> **REFLECTIVE QUESTION**
>
> - Imagine that you work in a language program that requires students to take a standardized English language test and achieve a certain score. One of your students asks you why students have to take this test when they are already taking English classes that include other assessments. How would you respond?

CHAPTER 4

From Curriculum Design to Implementation

At the implementation stage of curriculum design, you have already done a substantial amount of work. You have determined the reason for undertaking curriculum design and conducted a needs analysis. Yet implementing a curriculum requires a balance between keeping the big picture (i.e., curricular organization and goals) in sight while attending to smaller elements of the curriculum (i.e., ongoing decision making and planning day-to-day activities). An understanding of where curriculum designers and others fit into the big picture can also facilitate a sense of meaning for one's own work and encourage collaboration. In this chapter, we discuss ways of mobilizing stakeholders, administrators, faculty, and staff through communication, teaching and learning, and professional development as a new curriculum is put in place.

> **REFLECTIVE QUESTION**
> - Consider the following comment from a seasoned teacher: "I'm a little worried about curricular change. I've been teaching this way for 20 years, and it works." How would you address this concern in a way that validates the teacher's experience yet invites him or her to embrace new changes?

Communication

When either implementing a new curriculum or making changes to existing curricula, communication among all stakeholders is crucial. As Carroll (2007) stated,

> All of the social aspects regarding how a new program comes into being, how it is communicated to the various players, and how it changes as a result of interaction between people underlie the whole enterprise, and can make or break it. (p. 8)

It is important that key players involved in the curriculum are updated and informed about any new changes to the curriculum. Timely communication can help ensure a smooth transition and reveal the root of teachers' reluctance toward change (Nation & Macalister, 2010).

Consider an example that helps illustrate Carroll's (2007) statement. Recently, the university pathways program in which we teach merged two existing undergraduate programs into one. One change we needed to make was to determine which courses remained the same and which would be either phased out or merged with others, a decision that had significant implications for teaching assignments. After our curriculum committee conducted a needs analysis and worked extensively on the design of the new curriculum, we created a video that fully explained the new curriculum and how it compared to the previous one, the rationale for the changes made, and answers to previously voiced concerns. We sent the video to all faculty members with a link to a survey where they could ask questions about the planned changes. The committee collected the questions and prepared responses to share at the upcoming faculty meeting.

We believe that our approach was effective for several reasons. First, all faculty members, advisers, and staff had access to the same information at the same time. They could review the content and think about it before responding and asking questions, and our discussions of these major curriculum changes were able to continue outside the constraints of one face-to-face meeting where other important issues needed to be discussed. They were also able to access the video at any time and watch it as many times as they liked, so if they missed the in-person meeting, they would not have missed important information. The curriculum committee was able to acknowledge the feedback received and efficiently address specific concerns. When all faculty members were familiar with the big picture, they could better understand where their individual efforts fit in. The procedure we described provided a means for the designers to share information and receive feedback on how others' roles and responsibilities would be affected by the changes. It also provided a forum to gauge teachers' perceptions of the innovations so that the designers could formulate a response that addressed teachers' full experience, including their teaching expertise, changes in their workload, and their need for further information and/or training.

Teaching and Learning in the New Curriculum

Curriculum developments and changes may serve a broad range of purposes, yet student learning is always at the core. Once teachers begin teaching in a new curriculum, they should also conduct a more localized and specific needs analysis to determine the learners' needs and the resources available. The following questions can provide a good starting point and help teachers plan accordingly:

- What are the objectives for the course?
- How will the students reach these objectives?
- What resources do teachers and students need to meet them?
- What resources are currently available (e.g., textbooks, supplemental materials, classroom space, technology, syllabus, funding, mentors, coworkers, time)?

Many decisions in lesson planning and teaching are made on an ongoing basis, and the nature of ongoing decisions relates to the degree to which a curriculum is either product-oriented or process-oriented. According to Wette (2010), a product-oriented curriculum is organized around predetermined specifications that learners will reach as a result of instruction. In this type of curriculum, emphasis is placed on pre-course planning and positioning the teacher as the authority on the curriculum and the learners as receivers. On the other end of the spectrum, Wette describes a process-oriented curriculum in which the teacher and learners work together to negotiate a syllabus to address learner needs and preferences. The teacher is a facilitator and resource provider, and teachers and learners are considered collaborators.

While product-oriented approaches have been more common in TESOL, blending the two approaches is possible. For example, if learning objectives, a textbook, and assessments are established before the course begins, a teacher may be responsible for determining the course schedule and developing and carrying out lessons. In this case, teachers may collaborate with students to decide which types of learning activities to include and how much time to allocate to a given topic.

Additionally, Nation and Macalister (2010) describe a number of research-based principles to consider at this stage of implementation:

- generating interest and excitement in learning
- balancing focus on meaning, language, and fluency
- providing ample comprehensible reading and listening input
- increasing fluency
- producing speaking and writing in a variety of genres
- focusing on components of the language system (the sound system, vocabulary, grammar, and discourse)
- maximizing quality time spent using and examining English
- processing language deeply
- fostering positive attitudes toward English, its use, speakers, and the possibility of successful learning
- catering to students' individual learning styles

Examining how these principles are enacted in the classroom can help to create and maintain a productive environment for language learning within any language curriculum.

REFLECTIVE QUESTIONS

- Consider Nation and Macalister's (2010) list of principles presented above. How can instructors determine whether each and all of these elements are effectively implemented in their classrooms? For instance, how do you know if you have maximized the time in the classroom to use and examine English?

Textbook Selection

Textbooks and other teaching materials are a key consideration in achieving learning outcomes. While some teachers may gather materials from different sources for a course, many choose to use a published textbook. (For more on materials development, see Mann & Copland, 2015.) If there is a need for uniformity across classes or continuity across levels, or if teachers have limited time for material selection and development, it might be in the best interest of students to work with a textbook or textbook series. Some factors to consider when selecting a textbook include how well it fits with the learning objectives of the course in terms of skills, linguistic features, genres, or situations for language use. Most ESL textbooks, particularly those that target multiple skills, include a table of contents that details the scope and sequence of the material covered. Examining this page will provide information about themes, topics, specific recordings or texts, skills, grammatical features, vocabulary, learning strategies, types of activities, online components, and assessments that are included. From there, teachers can decide whether the book corresponds to the course learning objectives, teaching philosophy, and student population. Additional considerations are textbook availability and price.

> **REFLECTIVE QUESTIONS**
>
> - Think about a textbook that you have recently used either to teach or to learn a language. Which parts of the textbook were useful to you and why? Which parts were not useful and why? What are the advantages and disadvantages of using a textbook in an English language course?

Assessment

Finally, a well-designed course likely includes multiple types of assessment to provide information on student learning and achievement and areas for future growth. Diagnostic assessments provide information about students' relevant knowledge or skills at the beginning of a course. Formative assessments provide ongoing feedback about students' learning, which can be used to inform instruction; summative assessments at the end of the term provide information on whether students have met the course objectives.

Assessments can come from a variety of sources. Textbook series often offer assessments that correspond with the text. If the entire course is based on a textbook, this type of assessment may be sufficient. In many cases, an instructor or curriculum designer may develop their own assessments to demonstrate growth over time or determine the extent to which a learner is meeting the desired outcomes. (For more on assessment, see Cheng, 2015.)

Teacher Development

When implementing a new curriculum, one responsibility of curriculum planners and administrators is to support teachers' professional development. Professional development needs, including content knowledge, teaching methodology, assessment practices, and technical training, can be addressed in many ways. (For a more in-depth look at professional development, see Farrell, 2015.) Nonetheless, Crandall and Christison (2016) point out a trend in professional development for in-service teachers that moves away from brief decontextualized workshops offered to teachers and moves toward teachers creating their own opportunities to examine issues arising in their classrooms. They describe a sociocultural approach that embraces teachers' roles in their own learning and the local contexts in which they work.

Teacher development may take different forms. One form is action research, in which teachers investigate an area of their teaching through cycles of (1) identifying issues and planning and investigation, (2) carrying out an intervention, (3) observing and documenting the intervention in action, and (4) reflecting on and evaluating the intervention (Burns, 2010). Another way that teachers can engage in ongoing teacher development to meet the evolving needs of their classes is through reading and keeping up with developments in the field. A survey of adult ESL administrators and instructors in Canada found that the instructors who read peer-reviewed research articles reported a positive effect on their teaching (Abbott, Rossiter, & Hatami, 2015).

Professional development can also occur through learning communities, networks of teachers, and avenues for collaboration among colleagues (Crandall & Christison, 2016). As Fullan (2001) explains, while people in an organization are important during periods of change, it is the relationships between them that bring about results. Therefore, professional development is not only about developing individuals, but also about cultivating new relationships. Opportunities for interaction among teachers could be created through faculty and staff meetings, mentoring programs, or online forums. Tour (2017) provides an example of a personal learning network (PLN) in which a group of teachers initiated an online collaboration to advance their professional learning. Some meaningful outcomes of PLNs include the collection of resources, dialogue, collaboration, reflection, and socializing. A more informal approach to collaboration involves arranging a place and time for teachers to meet with one another face to face or virtually. Providing these types of supports is a means to increase teacher effectiveness and successful implementation of a curriculum.

Finally, a form of teacher development that can also inform future curricular change is reflection. Farrell (2013) defines reflective teaching as "examining what you do in the classroom and why you do it" and "thinking about the beliefs and values related to English language teaching and seeing if classroom practices are consistent with these beliefs and values" (p. 4). Farrell goes on to say that reflective teaching is important for informing practice because it provides teachers with information that they can use to make positive changes to their teaching. Taking a few minutes after each lesson to jot down notes about what worked, what could be improved, and next steps can inform the day-to-day implementation of the course and serve as a record to return to when evaluating and revising the curriculum. (For an excellent resource on reflective teaching that includes 80 practical reflection breaks, see Farrell, 2004.)

REFLECTIVE QUESTIONS

- Think about the professional development opportunities you have participated in. Which ones were the most useful and why? Which ones were not as useful and why?

Managing Change

Once a curriculum designer or committee has done the work of a needs analysis and design, implementing the new curriculum in a school or program would ideally go smoothly. Teachers would be eager to implement new curricular changes and feel optimistic that these changes will positively impact both their practice and student learning. While many teachers share these sentiments, Fullan (2001) reminds us that change is a double-sided sword: "on the one side, *fear, anxiety, loss, danger, panic*; on the other, *exhilaration, risk-taking, excitement, improvements, energizing*" (p. 1). Managing innovation and change is crucial to promoting the successful outcome you are working toward (Nation & Macalister, 2010), and planning ways to be attentive to and to manage the change process is crucial.

One possible difficulty brought on by change is what Fullan (2001) calls an "implementation dip," defined as "a dip in performance and confidence as one encounters an innovation that requires new skills and new understandings" (p. 40). Martel and Bailey (2016) provide an example in their description and analysis of the implementation of the American Council on the Teaching of Foreign Languages Integrated Performance Assessment (IPA) into a summer intensive language program, which replaced previously used midterm and final examinations. The program's associate director introduced this innovation and offered a series of professional development opportunities to support instructors in their use of IPAs. Interviews with the instructors revealed aspects of the intervention that they questioned and aspects that they supported. Despite multiple challenges that occurred, Martel and Bailey recognize positive steps taken in introducing this intervention as well as recommendations for the future, including involving instructors as well as administrators in decision making. While Fullan emphasizes that a dip is a normal part of a change process, it can be eased by keeping long-term goals in mind.

REFLECTIVE QUESTIONS

- How are classroom teachers uniquely qualified to contribute to curriculum design? What are the advantages and disadvantages of making the curriculum design process inclusive of many people?

CHAPTER 5

From Implementation to Evaluation

By this point in the curriculum design process, you have implemented the curriculum or curricular changes and are ready to ask questions about their effectiveness. Just as assessment is built into course design, an evaluation plan should be incorporated into curriculum design. In this chapter, we describe the tools that can help ensure the overall quality of the language program.

> **REFLECTIVE QUESTION**
>
> - The word *curriculum* has origins in the Latin word *currere* ("running" or "course"). What factors are important for making a curriculum run smoothly?

Defining Curriculum Evaluation

While the term *evaluation* can have a negative connotation, evaluating a curriculum is an informative component of curriculum development. It involves asking questions, collecting relevant data, and analyzing data to shed light on strengths and areas for improvement. Richards (2001) explains that evaluation can provide insight into how a curriculum is working and effectively achieving its objectives; what is occurring in classes; whether students, teachers, and others invested in the curriculum are pleased with it; and how the curriculum matches up to similar ones. He also states that once this information is collected, it can be used to make decisions and changes within the curriculum as needed. With these factors in mind, we must consider how to manage the evaluation process in a way that is beneficial and worthwhile for all involved.

Curriculum evaluation, similar to classroom assessment, can be either formative or summative. Nation and Macalister (2010) explain that distinctions between these two types of evaluation are based on the purpose (improvement vs. judgment), type of data collected (oriented toward individuals and process vs. oriented toward results or groups), how data are used (informing changes vs. determining adequacy), and how findings are presented (through discussion with relevant individuals vs. in a report). An example of a formative evaluation is a midterm questionnaire a teacher gives students to gauge their satisfaction in the course and make adjustments accordingly. An example of a summative evaluation is the process that a language program completes to gain accreditation from a recognized organization such as the Commission on English Language Program Accreditation (2016), which provides accreditation for postsecondary intensive English language programs and institutions in the United States and other countries around the world.

> **REFLECTIVE QUESTIONS**
>
> - What barriers might deter a teacher or language program from conducting a curriculum evaluation? Why might it be worthwhile to find ways of overcoming these barriers?

Using a Framework to Support Evaluation

Mertens and Wilson (2012) offer four main paradigms (or models) that can be used to guide educational evaluation. These models are helpful because they remind evaluators that there are many possible approaches that can shape the process of curriculum evaluation. The first paradigm is *postpositivist*, which relies mainly on quantitative research designs and data, including enrollment numbers and test scores. Mertens and Wilson state that a postpositivist evaluation often utilizes experimental design in which specific variables are examined. The second paradigm is *constructivist*, which employs qualitative (descriptive) methods to examine multiple values and perspectives. For instance, this paradigm illustrates how people experience and understand social phenomena and their world around them.

Mertens and Wilson's (2012) third paradigm is *pragmatic*, which makes use of quantitative and qualitative methods. Under a pragmatic paradigm, the focus is on producing evidence that can be used for a predetermined purpose, such as understanding the causes of absenteeism in order to improve student attendance. Finally, a *transformative paradigm* promotes social justice by focusing on marginalized groups and systemic power structures using a combination of numerical data and descriptive data. A transformative paradigm focuses on exposing and addressing inequalities to promote social justice. If questioning the status quo is the goal of an evaluation, Norris (2016) recommends engaging multiple stakeholders in the evaluation process.

To demonstrate how these paradigms can be applied to English language learning, Table 2 summarizes Mertens and Wilson's (2012) four paradigms and their foci. It also presents sample questions that may be asked in each paradigm and a list of possible sources of data and approaches to analysis. We would like to emphasize that one paradigm is not necessarily better than another; rather, what makes one useful is its relevance to the purpose of the evaluation.

Table 2. Paradigms for Sample Curriculum Evaluations

Paradigm	Focus	Sample questions	Data and analysis
Postpositivist	Objective data	What effect does a supplemental reading curriculum have on students' reading rate and reading accuracy?	• Reading rate and accuracy scores • Comparison of pre- and postreading rates and scores
Constructivist	People and their experiences in the real world	What do students think about online versus face-to-face courses?	• Focus group interviews with students who have taken both types of courses • Identification of commonly occurring themes
Pragmatic	Use and application	Is there a relationship between class size and student achievement?	• Samples of student work from classes of various sizes • Comparison of evaluations of student work based on rubrics
Transformative	Social justice	Are there differences in program graduation rates of students from different linguistic or cultural backgrounds? What contributes to these differences?	• Enrollment and graduation figures • Exit interviews • Questionnaires given to students upon exiting the program • Identification of similarities

Source: Based on Mertens and Wilson (2012).

REFLECTIVE QUESTIONS

- Which of these paradigms are most familiar to you? Why would it be beneficial to explore a less familiar paradigm?

Engaging in Curriculum Evaluation

Curriculum evaluation is a process, much like curriculum design and research. It begins with a specific question or purpose and ends with results than can then lead into another cycle of questions and investigation. Nation and Macalister (2010) summarize the steps involved in curriculum evaluation:

1. Discover the purpose and type of the evaluation.
2. Assess the time and money needed.
3. Decide what kinds of information to gather.
4. Gain the support of the people involved.
5. Gather the information.
6. Present the findings.
7. Apply what has been learned from the evaluation.
8. Do a follow-up evaluation. (p. 134)

The audience and purpose of an evaluation are important starting points because they influence the questions that will be asked, which in turn inform the methods used to collect and analyze the data and the ways in which the results are shared (Kiely & Rea-Dickins, 2005). For example, think about an evaluation prompted by prospective students who want to know about the preparedness of a program's graduates in pursuing their next steps. This evaluation would be different than one initiated by curriculum designers who want to know if the writing assignments in one level of a multilevel curriculum prepare students for the assignments in the next level or if they are too repetitive. While the first question highlights information about the effectiveness of a language program that would be shared with an audience outside of the program, the second question focuses on the ongoing work of a language program for an internal audience. Notably, both are driven by clear and focused questions.

Once you determine the guiding question in an evaluation, the next step is to choose appropriate data collection methodologies. Norris (2009) highlights the value in using multiple methods of data collection to understand both measurable outcomes and the factors that contributed to them. Data collected for evaluations may be either quantitative (e.g., test scores, questionnaires that include Likert scales) or qualitative (e.g., interviews and self-reports from teachers and students). There are many potential sources of data to inform the evaluation, including but not limited to the following:

- course evaluations completed by students
- course observations conducted by peers or supervisors
- journals and reflections by teachers
- teaching materials and assignments
- exams, assessments, and rubrics
- artifacts of student work
- interviews
- focus groups
- questionnaires
- audio or video recordings of classes

Each source of data may illuminate a different aspect of the curriculum, and several sources of data may be required to create a robust picture of the curriculum's efficacy. Once the data are collected, the analyses may include either statistical tests, an analysis of patterns, or a comparison of multiple data sources.

> **REFLECTIVE QUESTION**
>
> - Think about a language program you know well, and compose a couple of potential evaluation questions. Then use the list above to select some possible sources of data you could use to answer your questions. Which additional data sources would you like to add to the list?

Sharing Evaluation Results

Of all of the steps in the curriculum design process we have discussed thus far, presenting the results of a curricular evaluation may be the least familiar. Norris (2016) points out that while the field of language program evaluation is growing, publicly available evaluation reports are still lacking. One reason is because evaluation is a largely private endeavor that is meant for internal audiences. This point echoes one that we made earlier, that the audience and purpose of an evaluation determine the form the reporting will take. For example, you may share results through a memo of recommendations provided to the curriculum designers for revision, a presentation to faculty or administrators, or a written report published in an academic or professional journal. Regardless of the audience, Norris (2009) advocates for constructive relationships between language educators and evaluators. To meet this objective, he recommends including the following components of an evaluation report:

- background and contextual information about the program and curriculum
- information about stakeholders
- methods used in the evaluation
- reflections on the evaluation process
- recommendations for the program

An example of a curriculum evaluation is presented by Alhuqbani (2014), who conducted an evaluation of an English for specific purposes (ESP) course for police cadets in Riyadh, Saudi Arabia. The purpose was to

> evaluate the appropriateness and effectiveness of the English course and teaching at King Fahd Security College (KFSC) through the perspectives of teachers, current police cadets and former police cadets in terms of program density of hours, length, objectives, content and target learners . . . and contribute to the improvement of the teaching of English to police cadets. (p. 1001)

The evaluator/researcher administered questionnaires to English teachers in the program, current police cadets, and former police cadets, asking them the extent to which they agreed with a series of statements. He also wrote daily observations about comments he heard about the program. Alhuqbani reported the responses for each item on the questionnaires and used statistical analyses to determine which items the respondents answered similarly and which elicited different answers from the three groups. The discussion of the evaluation results highlights the importance of needs assessment for ESP programs, formulation of course objectives to be shared among all of the teachers, reevaluation of the duration of the program, and the need for periodical evaluation of the course. The conclusion of the report revealed several weaknesses of the ESP course and areas for improvement.

> **REFLECTIVE QUESTION**
>
> - What factors need to be taken into account when making evaluation results publicly available and why?

Navigating Sensitivity and Gaining Cooperation

Because evaluation data can reveal limitations and weaknesses of a program and instructors' performance, Nation and Macalister (2010) state that protecting participants' privacy and minimizing "face" threats throughout the process is extremely important. They also argue that an evaluation can be an "empowering and motivating activity" (p. 128) if evaluators gain the cooperation of other stakeholders involved and base the evaluation of a course on several assumptions. These assumptions include ensuring the course would benefit from evaluation, involving people who are able to make improvements, maintaining flexibility to allow for changes, and making sure any changes are useful. Nation and Macalister state that these assumptions can also be used to prioritize evaluation projects when time and resources are limited.

Though we began this chapter by acknowledging the negative connotation associated with evaluations, we presented approaches to curricular evaluation that promote well-functioning and effective language programs. Once an evaluation is complete, in order to make it worthwhile, curriculum designers should develop practical plans for follow-up, which then begins another cycle of the curriculum design process.

> **REFLECTIVE QUESTIONS**
>
> - Are there times in the program calendar that are a natural fit for evaluating how the curriculum is working? What types of events might occur during a teaching cycle that prompt you to take a look?

6

Recommendations and Conclusion

Throughout this book, we have described the most fundamental components of curriculum design. As we bring the book to a close, we would like to offer a few recommendations based on what we have learned in our experiences designing, maintaining, and evaluating language program curricula in diverse settings.

Curriculum Design Is Complex

We often emphasized throughout the book that curriculum design is a cyclical and nonlinear process. It involves collaboration and communication with many different people, takes a lot of organization and planning, and inevitably involves revisions and unforeseen challenges. As we reflected on our most recent experience working together on the undergraduate curriculum in our program, we realized that we shared an appreciation for what goes on behind the scenes and how much work is involved. We have come to recognize that successful curriculum designers need to be responsive, forward-focused, collaborative, and knowledgeable, as they play different roles as managers, decision makers, problem solvers, and educators. These roles may evolve throughout the process and change as the demands of curriculum design change as well, which makes curriculum design a complex yet stimulating professional experience.

There Is Not One Best Way

We have stated throughout the book that curriculum design is heavily dependent on the particular local context in which it exists. We have learned that what may work in one school or program may not work elsewhere, even if programs are similar in nature. With so many variables, there are unlimited possibilities and resources for designing, planning, implementing, and evaluating an English language curriculum, and thus there is not one best approach that will work in every educational setting. Instructors should remain flexible and acknowledge that they can reach out to others in the field or turn to published resources to benefit from a range of perspectives, ideas, and advice.

Curriculum Design Is Best Learned by Doing

As we thought about how we first learned about curriculum design, we realized that much if not most of what we learned about it was learned by doing. We believe that there are a few reasons for this. First, courses on curriculum design alone are not offered in all TESOL programs, so teachers and stakeholders who engage in curriculum design often receive little prior training. Another reason is that teachers may inadvertently find themselves in a curriculum designer role depending on the context in which they are teaching and contribute to decisions about courses, objectives, and perhaps the program of study. A final reason is that each foray into curriculum design will differ from previous ones and offer new opportunities for professional growth, as each experience is context-dependent. Nevertheless, the most basic principles of curriculum design can provide a starting point for teachers and stakeholders who have varying levels of experience working on language curriculum design. We encourage readers to seek opportunities to engage in the process and apply some of the principles we have described in this book to make positive changes to their language programs and courses.

Collaboration Is Valuable

Curriculum design is rarely an individual undertaking because so many different people are involved with a curriculum. If teachers are embarking on a curriculum design journey, they need to consider which attributes, skills, and knowledge they are already bringing along, what will be needed for the project, and the alliances that can be formed to get the work done. They should also consider building a team of colleagues who can bring particular strengths to the process. Sharing viewpoints, questions, and concerns with all people involved along the way ensures that one person's blind spots are compensated for by another's expertise. Working with colleagues can also make the process of curriculum design less daunting and more enjoyable.

Conclusion

Working to develop a new curriculum or implement tangible curriculum changes is difficult, yet we have both found the process to be extremely rewarding. We have truly enjoyed the sense of accomplishment we felt as we made concrete changes to our curriculum and took steps to improve teaching and learning for all involved. Furthermore, our experience has shown us that curriculum design is an excellent opportunity for professional development, and it has helped us think more critically about our teaching and our teaching philosophies. We hope that readers find the process as fulfilling and as engaging as we have and feel confident to tackle new tasks within the process of curriculum design.

References

Abbott, M. L., Rossiter, M. J., & Hatami, S. (2015). Promoting engagement with peer-reviewed journal articles in adult ESL programs. *TESOL Canada Journal, 33*(1), 80–105.

Alhuqbani, M. N. (2014). Teaching English to Saudi police cadets: An evaluation study. *Journal of Language Teaching and Research, 5*, 999–1008.

Auerbach, E. R. (1992). *Making meaning making change: Participatory curriculum development for adult ESL literacy*. Washington, DC: Center for Applied Linguistics.

Brown, H. D., & Lee, H. (2015). *Teaching by principles: An interactive approach to language pedagogy* (4th ed.). White Plains, NY: Pearson Education.

Burns, A. (2010). *Doing action research in English language teaching: A guide for practitioners*. New York, NY: Routledge.

Caplan, N. A., & Stevens, S. G. (2017). "Step out of the cycle": Needs, challenges, and successes of international undergraduates at a U.S. university. *English for Specific Purposes, 46*, 15–28.

Carroll, M. (2007). Creating a new curriculum: Leadership and communication. In M. Carroll (Ed.), *Developing a new curriculum* (pp. 1–10). Alexandria, VA: TESOL.

Cheng, L. (2015). *Language classroom assessment*. Alexandria, VA: TESOL.

Christison, M., & Murray, D. A. (2014). *What English language teachers need to know, volume III: Designing curriculum*. New York, NY: Routledge.

Commission on English Language Program Accreditation. (2016). *CEA standards for English language programs and institutions*. Retrieved from http://www.cea-accredit.org/images/2016_CEA_Standards.pdf

Council of Europe. (2001). *Common European framework of reference for languages: Learning, teaching, assessment*. Cambridge, UK: Cambridge University Press.

Crandall, J., & Christison, M. (2016). An overview of research in English language teacher education and professional development. In J. Crandall & M. Christison (Eds.), *Teacher education and professional development in TESOL: Global perspectives* (pp. 3–34). New York, NY: Routledge.

Cumming, A. (2009). Language assessment in education: Tests, curricula, and teaching. *Annual Review of Applied Linguistics, 29*, 90–100.

Farrell, T. S. C. (2004). *Reflective practice in action: 80 reflection breaks for busy teachers*. Thousand Oaks, CA: Corwin.

Farrell, T. S. C. (2013). *Reflective teaching*. Alexandria, VA: TESOL.

Farrell, T. S. C. (2015). *Language teacher professional development*. Alexandria, VA: TESOL.

Fullan, M. (2001). *Leading in a culture of change*. San Francisco, CA: Jossey-Bass.

Kiely, R., & Rea-Dickins, P. (2005). *Program evaluation in language education*. New York, NY: Palgrave Macmillan.

Kikuchi, D. (2017, January 6). Japan aims to overcome language, cultural barriers before 2020 Games. *Japan Times*. Retrieved from http://www.japantimes.co.jp

Lee, M. W. (2014). A participatory EFL curriculum for the marginalized: The case of North Korean refugee students in South Korea. *System, 47*, 1–11.

Mann, S., & Copland, F. (2015). *Materials development*. Alexandria, VA: TESOL.

Martel, J., & Bailey, K. M. (2016). Exploring the trajectory of an educational innovation: Instructors' attitudes toward IPA implementation in a postsecondary intensive summer language program. *Foreign Language Annals, 49*, 530–543.

Massachusetts Department of Education. (2005). *Massachusetts ABE curriculum framework for English for speakers of other languages*. Retrieved from http://www.doe.mass.edu/acls/frameworks/frameworks.html

Mertens, D. M., & Wilson, A. T. (2012). *Program evaluation theory and practice: A comprehensive guide*. New York, NY: Guilford Press.

Nation, I. S. P., & Macalister, J. (2010). *Language curriculum design*. New York, NY: Routledge.

Norris, J. M. (2009). Understanding and improving language education through program evaluation: Introduction to the special issue. *Language Teaching Research, 13*(1), 7–13.

Norris, J. M. (2016). Language program evaluation. *Modern Language Journal, 16*, 169–189.

Richards, J. (2001). *Curriculum development in language teaching*. Cambridge, UK: Cambridge University Press.

Richards, J. (2013). Curriculum approaches in language teaching: Forward, central, and backward design. *RELC Journal, 44*(1), 5–33.

TESOL. (2006). *PreK–12 English language proficiency standards.* Alexandria, VA: Author.

Tour, E. (2017). Teachers' self-initiated professional learning through personal learning networks. *Technology, Pedagogy, and Education, 26*(2), 179–192.

Wette, R. (2010). Product-process distinctions in ELT curriculum theory and practice. *ELT Journal, 65*(2), 136–144.

WIDA. (2012). *2012 amplification of the English Language Development Standards.* Retrieved from https://www.wida.us/standards/eld.aspx

Wiggins, G., & McTighe, J. (2005). *Understanding by design* (2nd ed.). Alexandria, VA: Association for Supervision and Curriculum Development.

www.ingramcontent.com/pod-product-compliance
Ingram Content Group UK Ltd.
Pitfield, Milton Keynes, MK11 3LW, UK
UKHW051259180426
11947UKWH00020B/1805